The Ladybird Key Words Reading Scheme is based on these commonly used words. Those used most often in the English language are introduced first—with other words of popular appeal to children. All the Key Words list is covered in the early books, and the later titles use further word lists to develop full reading fluency. The total number of different words which will be learned in the complete reading scheme is nearly two thousand. The gradual introduction of these words, frequent repetition and complete 'carry-over' from book to book, will ensure rapid learning.

The full-colour illustrations have been designed to create a desirable attitude towards learning—by making every child *eager* to read each title. Thus this attractive reading scheme embraces not only the latest findings in word frequency, but also the natural interests and activities of happy children.

Each book contains a list of the new words introduced.

W. MURRAY, the author of the Ladybird Key Words Reading Scheme, is an experienced head-master, author and lecturer on the teaching of reading. He is co-author, with J. McNally, of 'Key Words to Literacy'—a teacher's book published by The Schoolmaster Publishing Co. Ltd.

For use in schools, colourful work books, supporting material and apparatus based on Key Words is available. Write for details from the publishers:

WILLS & HEPWORTH LTD., LOUGHBOROUGH, Leics.

THE LADYBIRD KEY WORDS READING SCHEME has 12 graded books in each of its three series—'a', 'b' and 'c'. These 36 graded books are all written on a controlled vocabulary, and take the learner from the earliest stages of reading to reading fluency.

The 'a' series gradually introduces and repeats new words. The parallel 'b' series gives the needed further repetition of these words at each stage, but in different context and with different illustrations.

The 'c' series is also parallel to the 'a' series, and supplies the necessary link with writing and phonic training.

An illustrated booklet—'Notes for Teachers' —can be obtained free from the publishers. This booklet fully explains the Key Words principle and the Ladybird Key Words Reading Scheme. It also includes information on the reading books, work books and apparatus available, and such details as the vocabulary loading and reading ages of all books.

Book 11b

THE LADYBIRD KEY WORDS
READING SCHEME

The Carnival

by

W. MURRAY

with illustrations by

M. AITCHISON

Publishers : Wills & Hepworth Ltd., Loughborough
First published 1967   ©   Printed in England

Simon and John read that there was to be a carnival in their home town. They decided to join in the fun. They wanted to see the fun fair and take part in the procession.

To enter the carnival procession they could walk along in fancy dress, or else drive a car or lorry that had been decorated.

"We could get a lorry and find somewhere to keep it while we work on it," said John. "The father of one of my friends has a lorry he is not using. I'm sure he would let us have it for the carnival. We could keep it in a large building like a barn."

The two boys called on several of their friends to explain their idea and to ask for their help. All of them wanted to join in the fun. John telephoned about the lorry and was delighted to hear that they could have it. Then they had some more good luck. One of their friends had an uncle who was a farmer. When he heard of their plan, he arranged for them to use one of his barns.

"Now we need a good idea for our entry," said Simon.

7214 0023 X

The friends met in the barn to decide what to make for the carnival procession. John had brought the lorry and they were all pleased to see that it was a big one. They sat by it while they talked over different ideas for their entry.

After some time they decided to make a model of a space ship in flight. Two of them would dress up as astronauts and they would try to make it appear that one of these astronauts was walking in space near the space ship. "Let's draw a plan on that large white wall," said Simon.

One of Simon's friends could draw very well. He had some coloured chalks, and he started to use them on the wall. The others sat around watching as he worked on this drawing. First he drew the back of the lorry and then he drew the space ship on it. After this he put in the two astronauts. One was in the space ship, and the other seemed to be walking in space.

"How can we make the astronaut stay up like that?" asked one boy. "We must use some wire," said Simon.

Simon's friend used blue chalk for the background of his drawing. "We can paint the wires blue so that they will not be seen," he said. "It is a good idea to use a blue background," said John, "because the sky is blue."

"We must remember that there are two processions," said another of the boys. "One is in the early afternoon, and the other much later when it is dark. We should have lights to show up the space ship and the astronauts. There should also be flashing lights on the space ship."

"Let's make a list of all the things we need," said Simon. He got a piece of paper and a pencil and started to write. The others helped him with the list. Then he pinned it on the wall by the plan.

The next thing to do was to get the tools, wood, paint and other things needed for the work they were going to do. This took the rest of the day.

They all found that most people were glad to give them what they could. Everyone knew about the carnival and the procession. The money it would make was to help poor children and old people in need.

All the boys were soon hard at work on the space ship or the space suits for the astronauts. The lorry was to be decorated later.

Simon worked on the space ship with his friends. They had some pictures to help them. The ship was made of wood and cardboard but it looked real when painted silver and gold. The silver and gold colours showed up well against the blue background. Simon and his friend talked to each other as they worked. "We must be careful as we get in and out of the spaceship," said Simon. "It's not very strong and cardboard is easily damaged." "Yes," said his friend, "I won't mind using this ship for the carnival procession, but I would not like to shoot up into space in it." They fitted wires to hold the model in place on the lorry and then painted the wires blue.

The space suits for the astronauts were made of rubber and old clothes. Someone had given the boys some pieces of foam rubber which were very useful. They found that they could paint the home-made space suits with the silver paint they had, and that the paint dried quickly.

When the space ship and the space suits were ready, all the boys decorated the lorry. They gave the ship the name, 'Space Explorer' and painted it on a name-plate they had made.

One of the boys got into a space suit and climbed into the space ship. Then Simon put on the other space suit. He had to arrange himself so that it looked as if he were floating in space. He did this by holding on to some wires with his hands while one foot rested on the edge of a box which had been painted blue. The other foot was in the air. The wires and the box had been carefully placed so that they would not be seen easily. They were in just the right places to make it look as though Simon was not holding on to anything but floating in space.

Everyone agreed that the model was good enough for the procession. "We might win a prize," said John. "There are a lot of prizes to be won."

"If Peter and Jane were here they could be in fancy dress and join in the procession," said Simon to John. "Let's write and ask them to come."

Peter and Jane were delighted to hear from Simon and John about the carnival. Their mother and father agreed that they should both go, and that they should wear fancy dress.

"I want to go as a clown," said Peter. "I have always wanted to dress up as a clown." "I will be a fairy," said Jane. "I want to be a beautiful fairy. Let us make my dress now, mother." She knew that her mother liked making them things to wear.

Before long the fancy dress clothes were nearly ready. Peter put on his and then decided that he would wear a mask. "It is more fun to wear a mask," he said. "I know where there is an old one that I could have. It needs painting but I could do that myself."

Father came in as Peter started work on the mask. "You all seem to be having a lot of fun," he said. "Is there anything I can do to help?"

"Tell me how I look," said Jane. "Do I look like a fairy?" "Yes," answered her father. "You make a beautiful fairy and Peter will look like a real clown." Then he helped Peter to paint his mask.

It was fine weather on the day of the carnival. Peter and Jane were excited as they took their places in the procession. They walked with other children who were in fancy dress. Some of them had tins to collect money from the people in the crowd. There was a large crowd of men, women and children along each street. Many visitors had come to watch, as well as the people from the town. There was talking and laughing, and music from the bands.

The children who collected money had a busy time as nearly everyone put coins into the tins.

In front of Peter and Jane was a large float which had been decorated by the nurses at the hospital. Some nurses were on it, and a man in bed who was supposed to be ill. "That man does not seem to be very ill," said Jane to Peter. "No," answered her brother, "he is just pretending." Some of the people in the crowd threw money and flowers on to the hospital float as it went by.

Peter and Jane enjoyed the procession. They had to walk a long way but they found that the music from the band helped them along.

As John drove the lorry slowly along in the procession through the crowds he could see that the 'Space Explorer' interested many people. They had seen many pictures of space ships and astronauts, and had read much about them. He saw by the look on the faces of many children that they thought the space ship was exciting.

Not all of the boys watching were feeling like this. Some called out funny questions to Simon. "Is it cold up there?" asked one boy. Another said, "I hope that you get back all right."

Simon had to try hard to pretend that he was floating outside the space ship. It was not easy to stand on one foot for a long time, although he had wires to hold on to. Both he and the other astronaut found that the foam rubber made them hot. They were glad when the procession was over and they could take off their space suits and have a cold drink.

Then they went to find Peter and Jane to take them round the fun fair. They knew that there would be interesting and exciting things to do. They had promised to give their young cousins a good time.

Peter and Jane had a rest and put their fancy dresses away. Then they were ready to go round the fun fair with Simon and John.

They came first to the laughing man. He was not a real man but a model of a man, made of rubber. He had a funny face and he was made to move as though he were laughing. From inside him there came the sound of a man's laughter. Children thought that he was funny as he sat there moving and laughing. As they looked at him and heard him laugh, it made them laugh, too.

This rubber man was just outside the fun fair. The noise he made brought people to see what was happening. Then they went on into the fun fair. There were many children having a good time at the different side-shows.

"There's a lot to see," said Peter to Jane. "What are we going to do first?" They decided to go into the Hall of Mirrors. Simon paid for all four of them to enter. Jane had never been into a Hall of Mirrors before, and John explained to her what she was going to see.

The Hall was a very long room with glass mirrors of different kinds on the walls. There were many of these large mirrors. People were walking slowly round the room, stopping every now and again to look into them. Many of the people were laughing as they looked at themselves in the glass on the walls.

Jane stopped at the first mirror. In it she saw herself as a very tall and thin girl. It was the glass which made her look so different. Then she moved on to another mirror. In this one she looked very short and fat. "Oh, I do look funny," she said. "I can't help laughing at myself."

Peter was laughing at himself, too. He was looking in a mirror which made him seem very short and fat with a very small face. The next one made him look tall and thin with a very long face.

Simon and John were also enjoying themselves as they went round the hall looking into different mirrors. Now and again they called each other to come and look at something very funny. They were so interested that it made time go very quickly.

"Funny photographs!" called out a man at one of the side-shows. "Take home a funny photograph! No waiting!"

Simon and John walked over to see what was happening. Peter and Jane followed them. They soon saw what it was that was making the people laugh. A large picture of a monkey without a face had been painted on a piece of wood. A boy was standing behind this so that his face was in the place where the monkey's should be. It looked as though the boy was the monkey. A man was taking a photograph of this.

Next to the picture of the monkey was another piece of wood which had been painted to look like a doll in funny clothes. Again there was no face and this time a little girl had put her face in the place where the doll's should be. She was going to have her photograph taken next. Her mother had just paid the photographer.

The boys watched and then looked round to see more models without faces. "Come on, boys and girls," said the man. "Have your photographs taken! You can be what you like—cowboy, cowgirl, soldier, Indian, strong man, monkey, doll or gipsy."

Jane and the boys decided to have their photographs taken. They paid the man and asked him how long they would have to wait before they got them. "Only a few minutes," he said. "Stand where you like, and I'll take you now."

Simon stood behind the picture of a soldier. "How about this?" he asked the others. "Oh, yes," said Jane. "That's the one for you." Then the man took Simon's photograph.

"What about me?" asked John. They all laughed when they saw John as a strong man. "All right," he said to the man. "This will do for me."

Then it was Jane's turn. She chose to be a gipsy girl. Peter could not decide what to be. First, he wanted to be a soldier like Simon, then he thought he would be a cowboy. But at the last minute he chose to be taken as a monkey.

Soon the man had taken all four photographs. These were soon ready for the children to take away. The two big boys and Jane were pleased with their photographs. Peter couldn't stop laughing when he looked at his. "The boys at school will like this," he said.

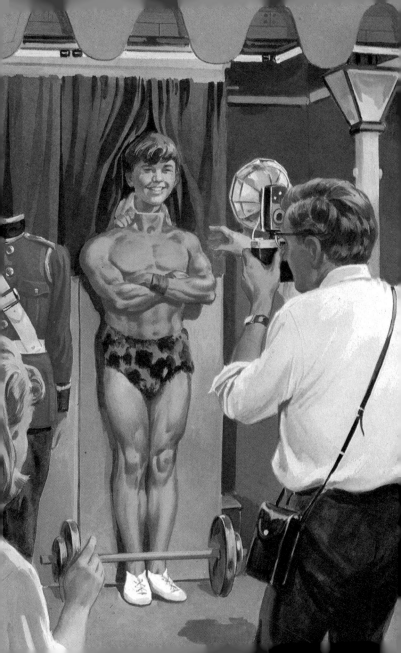

At another side-show a man was calling out, "Ring the bell and win a prize! A prize for anyone who rings the bell! It's easy!"

Near him some people were looking at a big boy who held a large hammer. The four children joined the crowd to watch. The boy put down the hammer and took off his coat. Then he took up the hammer and held it above his head. Suddenly he brought the hammer down hard to hit a wood block in front of him, This made another smaller block shoot straight up towards a bell some distance above his head. The small wood block did not ring the bell as it did not go up far enough to hit it. The boy tried again and again, but he could not make the bell ring. As the boy put on his coat to go away, Peter said to John, "You have a go. You were the strong man just now."

John paid the man, took off his coat and picked up the hammer. He hit the wood block hard and once again the smaller block shot straight up towards the bell. It came close to it but did not make it ring.

The man at the side-show called out again. "Come along the strong men! Ring the bell and win a prize!" John had another try. He came very close to ringing the bell but he could not quite do it. Then Simon tried. He hit the block as hard as he could several times but he did not quite ring the bell.

"Bad luck!" said Peter to his cousins. "I think it would take a very strong man to ring that bell." Just as he spoke, a very big man came along. He looked at the hammer and the bell and decided to have a try. He took off his cap and his coat and picked up the hammer. Several people stopped to watch. They wanted to see someone ring the bell and the big man looked very tall and strong. They expected him to be able to do it.

The big man suddenly hit the wood block with all his might. The bell seemed to ring at once. Six times the man brought the hammer down and the bell sounded every time. The children were delighted and waited to see the big man collect the prizes that he had won.

"Look over there," said Simon to the others. "It's the parachute jump. Let's go and see it."

A high platform had been made for the parachute jump, and there was a long ladder going up to it. They watched a young man go up the ladder and stand on the high platform while he put on the harness of an open parachute. This parachute was fastened to two long posts, but it could slide up and down safely. Then the young man jumped down towards the ground. He came down slowly because of the open parachute.

When he reached the ground the young man got out of the parachute harness. One of the men in charge made the empty parachute slide up until it reached the high platform again. Then it was the turn of someone else to jump.

"That looks exciting!" said Jane. "Yes," said John. "There is little danger, because the man on the ground could stop the parachute coming down if anything went wrong."

They watched a young girl go up the ladder for her turn, and noticed that one of the men went with her to fasten the harness safely.

"Let's all have a go!" said Peter.

Simon and John talked together about the parachute jump. "It is safe for us to jump, but what about Peter and Jane?" asked Simon. "The question is, what would their mother and father say if they were here?" "They like their two children to enjoy themselves, as long as they do it in safety," replied John quietly. "There is very little danger in this parachute jump. There are two men in charge and they are careful."

"Oh, do let us have a go," said Jane. "After all, we have been up in a helicopter." "I'm sure mother and father would let us go down," said Peter. "Perhaps they would," agreed Simon. "We will let you, then. I will look after Peter, and John will take care of Jane."

They did not have long to wait for their jumps. Peter went up the ladder first with Simon close behind him. The big boy took care that the straps were fastened and that everything was ready before his cousin jumped. After this Simon used the parachute then Jane and John had their turns. When John got Jane ready to go down, he was just as careful as Simon had been with Peter.

"Now for the Pet Show," said Jane, as they came towards a very large tent. "I want to see the Pet Show most of all. I do wish we could have brought our own dog." "Yes," said her brother. "I expect Pat would have won a prize."

As they entered the tent they heard the noise of animals and the singing of birds. The birds were near the entrance of the tent, so the children looked at these first. Several kinds of birds of many different colours were on show.

They came to the fish and found them very interesting. Many of them were goldfish but there were other fish they had never seen before. Some of these were valuable.

"Here are our friends the dogs," said John as they went on round the tent. He and Simon stopped to look at a very large dog. "This one must be the biggest one here," said Simon. "What a beautiful animal." Jane and Peter found a friendly puppy which kept jumping up at them.

The children moved on to see the cats. Many of these seemed not to notice the people looking at them. Some had even gone to sleep.

The two younger children owned rabbits so they were very interested in those on show. They spent some time looking at the rabbits and talked to several people about them. Then Peter saw a notice which read, 'THIS WAY TO CHILDREN'S CORNER.' They made their way there, followed by their two cousins.

There was a man in charge of Children's Corner and he spoke to them as they entered. "There is no need to be frightened," he said. "You can handle these animals if you want to. They are all used to children. Please don't give them food. We don't want them eating all day."

John asked Simon, "Why do you suppose they let children handle these pets?" Simon answered, "Perhaps the idea is to get children to like the animals and to be kind to them. Most children are kind to animals but there are a few who are not. Also, some children are afraid of animals."

There were many different kinds of pets in Children's Corner, and many children with them. Peter picked up a friendly little monkey and tried to talk to it. His sister found a very young donkey. Jane was very fond of donkeys.

"That's the biggest Pet Show I have seen," said Simon as they came out of the tent. "Yes, we spent a long time in there," said John. "I promised my mother that we would go to her stall," said Simon to Peter and Jane. "It is called the Home Made and Home Grown Stall. She and some of her friends have made or grown most of the food on the stall. I know the way there."

They were soon at the stall and found the boys' mother very busy. She told her sons that the food was selling well. "We are making a lot of money for the carnival," she said.

Peter and Jane had a look round the stall. They saw biscuits and cakes, jam, eggs and cream, toffee, dried fruit and fruit in bottles, tins of soup, flowers and ice-cream. Jane bought some cakes to take home for her mother. "Oh, how nice, they are still warm," she said in surprise. Peter also bought a bag of cakes. "These are to eat now," he told Jane. They enjoyed the cakes while their cousins were talking to their mother.

"There are still many things to see," said Jane.

HOME MADE AND HOME GROWN STALL

"Look, there's a Lucky Dip," called out Peter. He ran over to a stall which had three very large boxes in front of it. In each box were many parcels, most of them covered with coloured paper. They watched some other children having lucky dips before they had their own turns. "The bigger the parcel the more you have to pay," said Jane.

One small girl had a rubber fish in her parcel, another had a little doll. Some boys had a jigsaw puzzle, a toy watch, a model boat and a scrap book. Jane paid her money and took a red parcel. They all watched as she took out a pen, a pencil, some coloured writing paper and some envelopes. "Now I'll be able to write letters to you all," she said. Peter chose a bigger parcel. There was a box of paints and a painting book inside. These pleased him.

At first John said that he did not want to have a lucky dip, but Jane said that he should join in the fun. When he agreed he found a funny hat inside his parcel. The others laughed as he put it on.

Simon had a book about aeroplanes.

It was getting dark. Suddenly coloured lights in the trees round the fun fair came on. As the children looked up at the lights in the trees they could see a tree walk that had been made for the carnival. They went up steps which led to a platform made of planks of wood high up in a large tree. From there they walked along more planks of wood carefully put together to make a safe walking place from tree to tree. There was a handrail on each side of this tree walk.

Peter and Jane were delighted to be so high above the ground. They told Simon and John that they were not frightened and that they found it exciting. They all walked to a place between two trees from where they could see a long way. They held on to the handrail as they stopped to look at the lights of the town. From the fun fair below they could hear the sounds of music and people talking and laughing.

Suddenly a rocket shot up from the ground into the sky. By its light they could see a man climbing up a long ladder not far from the tree walk.

They could hear a man calling, "Come and see the flame diver! Come and watch the man without fear dive into the flames!"

"That sounds exciting," said John. "The flame diver must be the man climbing up that long ladder. He is climbing to a platform high above a large tank of water." "Where are the flames?" asked Peter. "I think they will pour something on to the water in the tank and set light to it," said Simon. "Yes," said John. "Then the man on the platform will dive into the water through the flames. Come on! We'll be just in time to see it if we go down now."

All four of them went quickly along the tree walk and down the steps to the ground. Then they joined the crowd of people round the tank of water by the ladder. The man in charge would not let anyone stand too close to the tank. By this time a light was shining on the man on the platform. He was standing quite still.

Then the man in charge poured something on to the water and set light to it. At once flames shot high into the air.

"Oh!" said Jane

"I hope there won't be an accident," said Peter quietly to Jane. "Oh dear," said Jane. "I don't like it." "Silence please!" called out the man in charge. "The flame diver is about to dive into the flames!" There was not a sound from the crowd as the man on the platform put his arms above his head. Then suddenly he dived towards the flames and disappeared into them.

What followed next was so quick that it was not easy to see what happened. The water splashed, the flames went out, and the head of the diver appeared above the water. It all seemed to happen at once.

"He's safe!" said Jane. "Yes, he's all right," said Peter. People clapped their hands and the children clapped too.

The diver climbed out of the tank and walked to the ladder which he started to climb. "He's going to do it again!" said Peter. He was quite right, for the diver made his way to the platform. The man in charge down below again set light to something he poured on to the water in the tank. "Silence, please!" he called. Then the diver splashed into the water and the flames disappeared again.

For the children the most exciting part of the carnival was the torchlight procession. Young people with torches held high walked along by the side of each float as the bands played. Peter and Jane found that they were walking near the float of the Queen of the Carnival. Everyone thought that the Carnival Queen looked very beautiful in her dress of red, blue and silver, and many people clapped her as she went by.

After the torchlight procession a large rocket shot up into the night sky. This was the start of the firework display. More rockets followed and then many other fireworks of different kinds were set off. The fun went on for a long time. Peter and Jane could not stay until the end, as their mother and father appeared after a while to take them home. The children were tired but very happy as they got into the car.

Simon and John stayed on until the firework display was over. Then there was more music, and dancing started. They joined in the dancing with some friends of theirs until they were tired. Then they started slowly on their way home. It had been a very happy Carnival Day.